# Cornerstones of Freedom

## The Story of

# THE MONTGOMERY BUS BOYCOTT

By R. Conrad Stein

Illustrated by Nathan Greene

CHILDRENS PRESS ®

CHICAGO

Library of Congress Cataloging-in-Publication Data

Stein, R. Conrad.
  The story of the Montgomery bus boycott.

  (Cornerstones of freedom)
  Includes index.
  Summary: Traces the events in the Montgomery,
Alabama, bus boycott which began in December, 1955,
and changed the course of the civil rights movement.
  1.  Montgomery (Ala.) — Race relations — Juvenile
literature.  2.  Segregation in transportation — Alabama —
Montgomery — Juvenile literature.  3.  Afro-American —
Civil rights — Alabama — Montgomery — Juvenile literature.
[1.  Montgomery (Ala.) — Race relations.  2.  Segregation
in transportation — Alabama — Montgomery.  3.  Afro-
Americans — Civil rights]  I.  Title.  II.  Series.
F334.M79N47  1986      976.1'47      85-31349
ISBN 0-516-04697-7

Copyright ©1986 by Regensteiner Publishing Enterprises, Inc.
All rights reserved. Published simultaneously in Canada.
Printed in the United States of America.

On a chilly afternoon a black woman named Rosa Parks boarded a bus after a long and tiring day. She deposited a dime in the fare box and took an empty seat behind the painted line that marked the "colored section" of the bus. It was December 1, 1955, in Montgomery, Alabama. Rosa Parks had no idea she was about to lead the vanguard of a revolution.

The bus rumbled along Cleveland Avenue and quickly began to fill up. After two stops all the seats in both the white and black sections were taken, and several black people stood in the rear aisle. At the next stop two white men climbed on board. The bus driver turned and called out to the seated black people at the back of the bus, "Give them your seats."

Three black passengers rose obediently, moved farther to the rear, and stood. They followed the custom observed on all Montgomery buses at the time. Not only were blacks obliged to sit in the rear of the bus, but, when the seats in the white section became filled, the blacks had to surrender their seats to white passengers. Furthermore, the law held that white passengers must not sit next to, or even across from, black passengers. So four blacks— two on each side of the aisle—had to rise to permit two whites to sit down. However, on this memorable afternoon, Rosa Parks refused to budge.

The driver twisted in his seat. "You, there," he said, pointing to Mrs. Parks. "You heard me, move to the rear."

Rosa Parks sat, stony faced, saying nothing. She was not a civil rights activist and had never dreamed of herself as a heroine. She was a forty-two-year-old seamstress who looked forward to spending a joyous Christmas with her family. Her lap was covered with boxes containing Christmas gifts. She was weary and her legs ached after an entire day of shopping. Also she was tired of suffering painful indignities on the buses of her hometown.

The bus driver cursed and jerked the hand brake. Red-faced with anger, he marched toward the seated passenger.

"I told you to move and I mean it!"

"No, I won't," Rosa Parks said softly.

A frozen silence fell upon the bus. Passengers, both black and white, dared not talk or stare at the scene. Only rarely did anyone challenge the age-old rules of Montgomery's transport system. Outside, car horns tooted as the stopped bus blocked traffic. Rosa Parks said nothing, but she would not move.

The frustrated driver hailed a police car and Rosa Parks was arrested. The passengers dismissed the event as just another minor incident on a city bus. No one realized that Mrs. Parks's defiance would make history. It was the opening drumbeat of a march that would shatter southern traditions and alter the course of America forever.

Rosa Parks lived in what is often called the "Jim Crow" South. It was profoundly different from the southern United States of today. The name "Jim Crow" dates back to a minstrel song popular before the Civil War. The term was used to describe the racial segregation laws enacted by southern states in the late 1800s.

It is difficult to imagine the day-to-day humiliation southern blacks had to endure during the Jim Crow era. Public water fountains were marked "whites" and "colored." Rest rooms were built in fours—two for blacks and two for whites. Public schools were segregated. On the railroads blacks rode in one car while whites rode in another. They also waited for their trains in separate waiting rooms and ate in separate restaurants. No detail was overlooked by the Jim Crow laws. Factory workers received their paychecks at different windows. Signs over laundries in the Deep South announced,

"We wash for white people only." A South Carolina law even forbade black and white cotton-mill workers from gazing out the same window.

There was little the blacks could do legally to challenge the system of segregation. Due to complex loopholes in registration laws most black southerners were denied the right to vote. Also, blacks who fought the old order faced the possibility of violence from militant white groups such as the Ku Klux Klan. The threat of a midnight lynching haunted any black considered by the militant whites to be a "troublemaker."

Nevertheless, many courageous blacks worked to overturn the Jim Crow establishment. They fought the system in courts, and, in some cases, openly defied the racist laws. But southern blacks were poor and had to worry more about making a living than about reforming the legal system. To effectively challenge the Jim Crow way of life, blacks needed a single, burning cause that would unite an entire community. The ideal issue emerged when Rosa Parks was arrested for disobeying Jim Crow laws on a public bus in Montgomery, Alabama.

Of all the indignities suffered by Montgomery blacks, none was more galling than their daily bus rides. On many routes white passengers were a rarity, but seats in the front half of the bus had to remain empty for them nonetheless. Meanwhile, during the rush hours, blacks stood crowded in the back of the bus gazing at rows of empty seats. Blacks made up more than 70 percent of the city's riders, yet there were no black drivers. And some white drivers seemed to delight in being abusive to blacks. One driver called a woman an "ugly black ape." A black man was shot to death because he demanded his fare back when he saw the bus was too crowded to ride.

Like electricity, word of Rosa Parks's arrest spread through Montgomery's black community. She was not the first black person to defy the city's Jim Crow rules on the buses. In the past year three others, all women, were jailed for refusing to surrender their seats to white passengers. Rosa Parks, however, knew an influential leader in the black community named E. D. Nixon. To take advantage of black anger toward the bus system, Nixon formulated a plan and hurried it into action. Mrs. Parks was arrested on a Friday. Nixon proposed that all blacks boycott the city's buses on the following Monday. At first the plan had limited ends. Nixon urged blacks to shun bus travel for one day only. He hoped a one-day action would show the city that the black community demanded better treatment.

Most people believed the boycott would fail. Blacks worked in far-flung areas of the city. They held low-paying jobs and often supported large families. Missing a day's wages because they could not take the bus to work would be disastrous for their family budgets. Still, plans for the Monday boycott went on. Leaflets were printed and circulated in the streets. The boycott was announced in Sunday church services and newspapers.

It was still dark on Monday morning when some of
E. D. Nixon's followers stood at a bus stop on Cleveland Avenue. Anxiously they waited for the first bus
to arrive. They believed that if at least two out of
three black passengers refrained from taking the
buses that morning the boycott would be a success.
At 5:00 A.M. a bus rumbled down the street. It held a
half dozen whites—but no blacks. At 5:15 another
bus passed. It was practically empty; again there
were no black passengers. Bus after bus rolled past
with no blacks aboard. On that historic morning the

sun rose on a new Montgomery. Normally, buses during the rush hour were crammed with black people, all of them sitting or standing in the rear. But on December 5, 1955, no blacks were seen anywhere on Montgomery's buses. E. D. Nixon was stunned. His one-day boycott was almost 100 percent effective.

Equally remarkable were the ingenious ways blacks used to get to work or school that morning. At the time few Montgomery blacks owned cars, but those who did organized car pools. Miraculously those car pool arrangements were made almost overnight. Black-owned taxi companies gave special reduced fares to boycotters. Many blacks walked to work even though that might mean a five-mile hike in the cold weather. Others peddled bicycles, and a few even rode mules to their jobs. A black minister stopped his car to give one frail, elderly lady a ride. He asked the woman if she were tired and if she really would prefer to take the bus. Her now famous reply gave the black community strength during the difficult months to come. The woman said, "My feet are tired, but my soul is at rest."

The astonishing success of the one-day boycott encouraged the leaders to attempt an even bolder plan. On Monday evening E. D. Nixon hastily called a community meeting at a local church. So many people showed up that an overflow crowd of three to four thousand had to listen to the proceedings from the church lawn. Nixon suggested to this throng that the boycott continue until the bus company agreed to certain demands of the black community. The crowd roared its approval. Nixon then introduced a young minister who was new in town and virtually unknown among Montgomery's churchgoing public. The people fell silent as the Reverend Martin Luther King, Jr., took the podium.

Only a few hours earlier the twenty-seven-year-old minister had decided to join the boycott movement. He had no prepared speech to give to this mass audience. Yet he delivered an address that witnesses claimed was spellbinding. He alternately coaxed the crowd into moments of rapturous silence, and then had them standing on their feet giving a thunderous ovation. In his book *Stride for Freedom,* King recalled some of what he said:

"We are here this evening to say to those who have mistreated us for so long that we are tired— tired of being segregated and humiliated; tired of being kicked about by the brutal feet of oppression.... For many years we have shown amazing

patience. We have sometimes given our white brothers the feeling that we liked the way we were being treated. But we come here tonight to be saved from that patience that makes us patient with anything less than freedom and justice."

King's speech that night established the man and his destiny. The Montgomery bus boycott was the first mass attack on the old segregationist South. It was also the political awakening of one of the most influential Americans of the twentieth century.

Martin Luther King, Jr., was born in Atlanta, Georgia, in 1929. He grew up stung by the everyday pains of life in the Jim Crow South. He attended

segregated schools and worshiped in segregated church services. Following his father's profession, he decided to enter the ministry. Unlike most southern preachers, he received his theological training in Boston. An avid reader, he marveled at how religion, literature, and philosophy had altered people's thinking through the ages. He was moved by the works of Mohandas K. Gandhi, who led millions in nonviolent protest against the British colonial occupation of India.

Through the power of his personality and the clarity of his ideas, the leadership of the bus boycott swung to Martin Luther King. The young minister

insisted that all protests be nonviolent. He reminded the people that Jesus Christ suffered oppression, but forgave His oppressors. To close his memorable speech the first night of the boycott, King said:

"If you will protest courageously, and yet with dignity and Christian love, when the history books are written in future generations, the historians will have to pause and say, 'There lived a great people—a black people—who injected new meaning and dignity into the veins of civilization.' This is our challenge and our overwhelming responsibility."

An excited group of people left the church that Monday night in December. For the first time, the blacks of Montgomery were united in a movement against the humiliation they suffered. And they had an inspirational leader in Martin Luther King. But they faced a stubborn foe—the Jim Crow laws and the attitudes of the Old South.

On January 16, 1956, *Time* magazine reported, "The Montgomery, Alabama [bus boycott] last week entered its second month, and was still 95 percent effective. Rallies were held twice a week in Negro churches, where overflow crowds gathered to receive the latest information on car pool schedules. . . ." The *Time* article was the first mention in a national magazine of the quiet revolution going on in Montgomery. Mass protests against Jim Crow traditions were a curiosity in the American South during the mid-1950s. In its first few weeks the boycott drew the attention of the state of Alabama. Next, all eyes in the South were upon it. Soon the entire nation wondered who would endure in Montgomery—the protesters or the Jim Crow establishment.

To the white citizens of Montgomery the boycott was at first a nuisance. They were unaccustomed to seeing out-of-town reporters and photographers

milling about the streets. Most whites thought (or hoped) that the movement would fail and things would soon return to normal. One man told a writer from the *New York Times*, "Frankly, I'll tell you, I think the [blacks] will just get right back into them buses like they always done before . . . and they'll move right to them back seats like always."

As the boycott continued, Montgomery's blacks adjusted to going about their business without the use of buses. A car pool of two hundred vehicles took men and women to and from their jobs. Negro taxi companies ran special routes during the rush hours

and served as makeshift buses. Some black families repaired fifty-year-old buggies and moved through the streets behind teams of clopping horses.

Soon the boycott accomplished precisely what its leaders hoped it would. It squeezed profits out of the bus company and hurt business downtown. Without black passengers the buses ran virtually empty. The bus company was forced to raise fares from ten to fifteen cents a ride. White store owners complained that blacks no longer came downtown to shop. Because of the boycott they did their shopping in neighborhood stores.

However, the boycott fueled the fires of racial hatred in Montgomery. The Reverend Mr. King and his wife, Coretta, received angry letters, and an anonymous phone caller warned, "Listen, nigger, we've taken all we want from you; before next week you'll be sorry you ever came to Montgomery."

On the evening of January 30, 1956, Mrs. King entertained a lady friend in her home. Her husband was conducting a function at church. Mrs. King had just put her baby to bed when she heard something thump against the front porch. It sounded like a

brick. Suddenly the thought flashed in her mind: *What if it's a bomb?* Mrs. King and her companion rushed toward the rear door. A terrifying explosion rocked the house.

Martin Luther King hurried home to find an angry throng of black neighbors ringing his house. No one in the King household had been injured, but the crowd was in a furious mood. Some of the men were armed with pistols. Montgomery's mayor and police chief were on hand, but they feared they could not control the outraged blacks.

In his book Mr. King recalled what he said to the people to calm this dangerous situation. "We cannot solve this problem through retaliatory violence. We must meet violence with nonviolence. Remember the words of Jesus—'He who lives by the sword will perish by the sword.'" He ended this impromptu speech on the steps of his shattered porch with the words, "Remember, if I am stopped, this movement will not stop, because God is with the movement. Go home with this glowing faith and this radiant assurance."

It was another triumph for Martin Luther King. Probably no other man in the city could have prevented a race riot from breaking out that night.

The bombing incident actually strengthened the resolve of the black community. The boycott leaders drew up a list of demands and declared that blacks would stay off the buses until those demands were met. The demands included integrated seating and the hiring of black drivers. To these conditions the bus company and the city answered with an unqualified "No!"

Spring came, followed by a long hot summer. Neither side was willing to give in. The city and state governments tried a series of harassing tactics

aimed at demoralizing the boycotters. Car pool drivers were stopped by police and ticketed for the most minor traffic offenses. A local judge ordered the Negro taxi companies to cease acting as makeshift buses. Martin Luther King and other boycott leaders were indicted for violating an obscure state conspiracy law.

Victory finally came for the blacks of Montgomery, but they achieved their triumph in court rather than on the streets. In the 1950s the U.S. Supreme Court began to strike down the South's ancient

racist laws. A landmark 1954 case held that segregated schools violated the Constitution. Practice and
law were two different things, however, as schools in
both the South and the North remained segregated
for years after that Supreme Court decision. Still,
one by one, Jim Crow laws fell in front of federal
judges. Finally, on November 13, 1956, almost a
year after Rosa Parks's historic bus ride, the
Supreme Court quietly declared that segregated
seating in buses was unconstitutional. The black
people of Montgomery had won at last!

In December 1956, newspaper reporters and
photographers again descended on Montgomery.

*Time* magazine wrote of the occasion:

"On a foggy warm morning last week the Negro boycott against the Montgomery, Alabama city bus lines came to an end. . . . The Negroes had won their fight: they rode unsegregated in the Confederacy's birthplace. Desegregation still had a long way to go, but after Montgomery, Jim Crow would never again be quite the same."

The boycott leaders, including E. D. Nixon and Martin Luther King, climbed aboard buses and took seats at the front as newsreel cameras recorded the event and reporters scribbled notes. King sat beside a white Montgomery minister who had supported the bus boycott. All over the city bus passengers were ignoring color lines for the first time in Montgomery's history.

With little fanfare Rosa Parks waited at a bus stop. Her impulsive defiance of Jim Crowism had started this revolution almost a year earlier. After her arrest for refusing to give up her seat, she was fined ten dollars, which she refused to pay. Now, when the bus arrived, she boarded and finally took a seat of her choice.

To the surprise of many southerners, most white passengers accepted the changeover with good humor. One white man, noticing two blacks sitting in front of him, smiled and said, "I see this isn't going to be a white Christmas." One of the black passengers returned his smile and answered, "That's right." Everyone on the bus chuckled.

The Montgomery bus boycott was the first step in the destruction of a system that had heaped abuse upon black southerners for almost a century. In the decade following the boycott, many dedicated blacks and whites worked together to tear down laws that treated blacks as second-class citizens. By the late 1960s the Jim Crow laws all over the South had crumbled.

Leading the attack on the old order was the Reverend Martin Luther King. After the Montgomery bus boycott he launched a nonviolent protest movement that spread even to the North, where a more subtle form of Jim Crowism existed. King's greatest triumph came in August 1963, when he led 200,000 people on a peaceful march in Washington, D.C. But in spite of King's dedication to peace he

was often the target of violence. He was stabbed in New York City and stoned in Chicago. He was also the subject of a vicious FBI investigation. Finally an assassin gunned him down on April 4, 1968.

Martin Luther King is buried in Atlanta, Georgia, the city of his birth. On his gravestone are the words of an old Negro spiritual. They are the same words he uttered on that shining day in Washington, D.C.: "Free at last, free at last, thank God Almighty, I'm free at last."

## About the Author

R. Conrad Stein was born and grew up in Chicago. He enlisted in the Marine Corps at the age of eighteen and served for three years. He then attended the University of Illinois where he received a bachelor's degree in history. He later studied in Mexico, earning an advanced degree from the University of Guanajuato. Mr. Stein is the author of many other books, articles, and short stories written for young people.

Mr. Stein now lives in Chicago with his wife, Deborah Kent, who is also a writer of books for young readers, and their daughter Janna.

## About the Artist

Nathan Greene is a graduate of the American Academy of Art in Chicago, where he studied Fine Art and Illustration. He lives in Clarendon Hills, Illinois, and enjoys backpacking, running, and, of course, art.